My Emotions
Mis emociones

CALM
TRANQUILO

A Crabtree Roots Book
Un libro de Las Raíces de Crabtree

AMY CULLIFORD
Traducción de Pablo de la Vega

Crabtree Publishing
crabtreebooks.com

School-to-Home Support for Caregivers and Teachers

This book helps children grow by letting them practice reading. Here are a few guiding questions to help the reader with building his or her comprehension skills. Possible answers appear here in red.

Before Reading:

- What do I think this book is about?
    - *This book is about how to feel calm.*
    - *This book is about what feeling calm looks or feels like.*
- What do I want to learn about this topic?
    - *I want to learn what makes people feel calm.*
    - *I want to learn what feeling calm looks like.*

During Reading:

- I wonder why...
    - *I wonder why we smile when we are calm.*
    - *I wonder why baths make people calm.*
- What have I learned so far?
    - *I have learned that drawing can make you feel calm.*
    - *I have learned that people sit when they are calm.*

After Reading:

- What details did I learn about this topic?
    - *I have learned that there are many ways you can feel calm.*
    - *I have learned that you can think things through when you are calm.*
- Read the book again and look for the vocabulary words.
    - *I see the word* ***drawing*** *on page 4 and the word* ***music*** *on page 8. The other vocabulary words are found on page 14.*

What makes you **calm**?

¿Qué te hace sentir **tranquila**?

Drawing makes me calm.

Dibujar me ayuda a estar tranquila.

I sit when I am calm.

Me siento cuando estoy tranquilo.

Music makes me calm.

La **música** me tranquiliza.

I can think when I am calm.

Puedo pensar cuando estoy tranquilo.

A **bath** makes me calm.

Darme un **baño** me tranquiliza.

I **smile** when I am calm.

Sonrío cuando estoy tranquila.

What makes you calm?

¿Qué te hace estar tranquilo?

Words to Know
Palabras para conocer

bath
baño

calm
tranquila

drawing
dibujar

music
música

smile
sonrío

40 Words

What makes you **calm**?

Drawing makes me calm.

I sit when I am calm.

Music makes me calm.

I can think when I am calm.

A **bath** makes me calm.

I **smile** when I am calm.

What makes you calm?

39 palabras

¿Qué te hace sentir **tranquila**?

Dibujar me ayuda a estar tranquila.

Me siento cuando estoy tranquilo.

La **música** me tranquiliza.

Puedo pensar cuando estoy tranquilo.

Darme un **baño** me tranquiliza.

Sonrío cuando estoy tranquila.

¿Qué te hace estar tranquilo?

My Emotions

CALM

Mis emociones

TRANQUILO

Written by: Amy Culliford

Designed by: Rhea Wallace

Series Development: James Earley

Proofreader: Ellen Rodger

Educational Consultant: Marie Lemke M.Ed.

Photographs:
Shutterstock: Juan Pablo Gonzaález: cover; ZouZou: p. 1; ESB Professional: p. 3, 14; LightField Studio: p. 5, 14; Africa Studio: p. 8, 14; Newman Studio: p. 9, 14; Chz_mhOng: p. 10, 14; narikan: p. 11, 14; Rusian Shugushev: p. 13

Crabtree Publishing

crabtreebooks.com 800-387-7650

Printed in Printed in China/082022/FE052422CT

Published in Canada
Crabtree Publishing
616 Welland Ave.
St. Catharines, Ontario
L2M 5V6

Published in the United States
Crabtree Publishing
347 Fifth Avenue,
Suite 1402-145
New York, NY, 10016

Library and Archives Canada Cataloguing in Publication
Available at the Library and Archives Canada

Library of Congress Cataloging-in-Publication Data
Available at the Library of Congress

Paperback: 9781039624511
Ebook: 9781039625358
Epub: 9781039624931